ISBN 978-1-330-47359-7
PIBN 10066468

This book is a reproduction of an important historical work. Forgotten Books uses state-of-the-art technology to digitally reconstruct the work, preserving the original format whilst repairing imperfections present in the aged copy. In rare cases, an imperfection in the original, such as a blemish or missing page, may be replicated in our edition. We do, however, repair the vast majority of imperfections successfully; any imperfections that remain are intentionally left to preserve the state of such historical works.

1 MONTH OF
FREE
READING

at
www.ForgottenBooks.com

By purchasing this book you are eligible for one month membership to ForgottenBooks.com, giving you unlimited access to our entire collection of over 700,000 titles via our web site and mobile apps.

To claim your free month visit:

www.forgottenbooks.com/free66468

English
Français
Deutsche
Italiano
Español
Português

www.forgottenbooks.com

Mythology Photography **Fiction**
Fishing Christianity **Art** Cooking
Essays Buddhism Freemasonry
Medicine **Biology** Music **Ancient
Egypt** Evolution Carpentry Physics
Dance Geology **Mathematics** Fitness
Shakespeare **Folklore** Yoga Marketing
Confidence Immortality Biographies
Poetry **Psychology** Witchcraft
Electronics Chemistry History **Law**
Accounting **Philosophy** Anthropology
Alchemy Drama Quantum Mechanics
Atheism Sexual Health **Ancient History**
Entrepreneurship Languages Sport
Paleontology Needlework Islam
Metaphysics Investment Archaeology
Parenting Statistics Criminology
Motivational

The Verbal Accent
in Russian.

Dissertation

presented to the

Philosophical Faculty of the University of Freiburg, Switzerland,

for the

degree of doctor of Philosophy,

in June 1896.

By

Alexander William Herdler,

late Instructor in Modern Languages, Princeton University, Princeton, N. J.

Leipzig und Wien,

Verlag von Raimund Gerhard

(vormals Wolfgang Gerhard).

1898.

Introduction.

It is a generally recognized fact, that the primitive Slavonic accent is of primary importance in the reconstruction of the Indo-European accent. The Ur-Slavonic accent has experienced a certain displacement owing as Sobolevskij [1] states "to the disappearance of the semi-vowels ъ, ь and of i at the end of words and to the influence of the nominal and verbal forms upon each other." Of the Slavonic languages, Polish, Bohemian and Sorbish have a fixed accentuation; Russian, Serbian, Slovenian and Bulgarian are characterized by their movable accent. Fluctuating accent was also peculiar to the Ur-Slavonic accent and can be reproduced by comparing the modern Slavonic tongues. „Die Betonung des Altbulgarischen kennen wir nicht, dieser Schaden wird aber dadurch beseitigt, dass sich aus den modernen slavischen Dialekten, vor allem aus dem Russischen und Serbischen der urslavische Akzent z. T. rekonstruieren lässt. Da eine getrennte Entwickelung dieser Dialekte stattgefunden hat, so darf man dem erschlossenen urslavischen Akzent grösseren Wert beilegen als dem litauischen; denn es zeugt die Übereinstimmung zwischen Russisch und Serbisch für das Urslavische, das der indogermanischen Sprache viel näher liegt als das heutige Litauisch." [2] From the fact that Serbian and Slovenian have still the falling and rising quality of the accent

---

[1] cf. Лекціи по исторіи русскаго языка 243.
[2] cf. Hirt: Der indogermanische Akzent 15.

and that Russian has the falling accent in the dissyllables óro, ólo, ére, éle and the rising accent in oró, oló, eré, elé it is inferred that the Slavonic accent had the same accent qualities.[1]) The accent[2]) in Russian does not fall upon any particular syllable, but varies in position being placed upon the root, the prefix, the suffix and even upon flectional endings of a word. It follows that logical principles and even homonyms of different meanings and gender are not distinguished by the accent. While on the one hand, words of a certain ending, especially those in -ніе, -ность, -ство and -тель are striving to unify their accentuation, others are shifting it to a new place without an apparent reason. The three Russian dialects, Great-, Little- and White-Russian often disagree in their accentuation. Little-Russian where it is spoken side by side with Great-Russian has in many cases adopted the latter's accentuation and again where the Little-Russians (Ruthenians) come in contact with the Poles as in Galicia, their language shows a marked tendency towards paroxytonization. The Little-Russian accent is perhaps more conservative than the Great-Russian, for the latter must certainly, have been influenced by the initial accentuation of the Finish tongues with which it came into early contact. A considerable part of the Great-Russians are russified Fins as is proved by their physiognomy and the geographical nomenclature of their territory. This influence may not have been as strong as for instance in English in which Norman-French words have gradually changed their accent in agreement with the principles which governed the Anglo-Saxon. Words like vertú, parlemént are now accented vírtue, párliament. For the purpose of reconstructing the Ur-Slavonic accent, Serbian and

---

[1]) cf. Leskien, Untersuchungen I 550 ff.

[2]) Comp Brandt: Лекціи по исторической грамматикѣ русскаго языка 101 ff., and Начертаніе славянской акцентологіи 11 ff. Sobolevskij: Лекціи по исторіи русскаго языка 23 and. Гротъ: Филол. разысканія 408 ff.

Russian are the most valuable languages. The latter is
deficient in one point, it has lost the quantity which is
still preserved in Serbian, Slovenian and Bohemiän. Bulgarian until lately had also a fixed quantity and the Mace-
donian dialects have still preserved remnants of long syllables.[1]) The accented syllables in Russian are a little
longer (about 2 moras) than the unaccented ones (1 mora)
but this phenomenon is more of a rhetorical character[2])
and stands in no connection with the Ur-Slavonic quantity. The pre-tonic syllable receives an almost impercep-
tible secondary accent in Russian while in Serbian the
post-tonic syllable bears this accent. Whilst Russian
thus lacks an essential element, i. e. quantity, for the
determination of the primitive Slavonic accent, Serbian
"gewährt für unsere Aufgabe die reichste Ausbeute, da es
die alten Betonungsverhältnisse fast nach jeder Seite un-
verändert erhalten hat. Es lässt sich nicht nur der Sitz
des Akzentes feststellen, sondern auch die (Quantitäten)
Qualitäten der Betonung lassen sich aus Quantitätsverände-
rungen durchgehends bestimmen, wobei sich eine fast völlige
Gleichheit mit dem Litauischen ergibt."[3]) With regard
to its accentuation, Serbian falls into the Western and Eastern
dialects. The Western or ča-dialects (ča = what) have
retained the original seat of the Ur-Slavonic accent whereas
in the Eastern or što-dialects (što = what) it has moved
one syllable to the beginning of the word. From this
follows that the final syllable is always unstressed. In
both dialects, the originally long quantities: a, ě, i, u, y,
ą, ę, or, ol, er, el, ьr, ъr, ьl, ъl are varyingly long or
short. Leskien in his "Untersuchungen über Quantität
und Betonung in den slavischen Sprachen", I, 24, has thus
formulated the respective rules: "Die in der ursprüng-
lichen Hochtonsilbe stehenden alten Längen werden 1. ver-

---

[1]) cf. Oblak, Archiv XV. 306.   [2]) cf. Brandt: Лекціи 100.
[3]) cf. Hirt: D. indogerm. Akzent 75.

kürzt, wenn ursprünglich der Ton steigend war und 2. erhalten, wenn ursprünglich der Ton fallend war." The
rising accent corresponds to the sharp (rude intonation,
Stosston), and the falling to the soft (douce intonation,
schleifend) accent in Lithuanian. Before the accent, the
old quantities remain intact. The old Serbian accent is
preserved in those words in which it originally bore upon
the first syllable. It is marked ˵to designate the brevity
of the stressed syllable and ⌃ is the mark for the long,
stressed syllable which kept its original quantity because
the tone was falling. The mark ˵therefore designates
both the originally short, stressed syllable and the originally
long, stressed syllable which was shortened if the accent
was rising. Both ˵ ⌃ are now falling: â (ā) = ăa, à (ă) =ăa.
While the old accent ˵ ⌃ which remained in its original
position is falling, the new secondary accent is rising. The
mark ´ is used to specify the long accent and ˋ characterizes
the short accent: á = aá, à = aǎ. Both may strike any
syllable except the last. "The falling accent has, as a
rule, kept its original position and quantity; the rising
accent has taken the place of an older falling accent whose
primary position was upson the following syllable, f. i.:
gláva > glāvà, govòriti > govorìti." [1])
   The originally long syllable following ˋ and ´ is therefore either long or short according as its accent was falling or rising, as Leskien has proved. With the accen-
tuations ´ or ˋ we find the original accent on the following
syllable. In Serbian, the accentuation is therefore either
original, old: Falling ⌢, ⌣ or secondary, new: Rising ⊥
⌣. The numerons reconstructions which I have made will
illustrate the shift which the old Serbian accent has car-
ried out. In Serbian, the accent in its old form does not
always agree with the Russian accent and this fact will be
noticed in each case. — In the following pages are treated

---

[1]) cf. Rešetar, Archiv, XVII, 192.

the changes which the accent of the simple and those verbs undergoes which are felt to be simple verbs. Of the verbal forms, the present passive participle in -мый, -мая, -мое, the past gerund active in -въ, -вши and the past active participle in -вшій, -вшая, -вшее are disregarded for they retain, almost without an exception, the accentuation of the infinitive. Questions concerning the Indo-European accent will not be touched upon, my immediate object being to present the material in a comprehensive form. The reader's attention is called in a footnote to the few verbs treated by Dr. Hirt in his very valuable book: "Der indogermanische Akzent". The comparisons with Serbian and Little-Russian are given as far as they could be obtained from the only two monographs treating of the verbal accent of the respective languages, viz.: Akcenti u glagola by Damičić and: Über den Accent der Verba im Kleinrussischen, Archiv II, 289 ff., by Hankiewicz. As regards the verbal accent of Slovenian and modern Bulgarian, such representations are wanting and therefore these languages could not be used for the purpose of this thesis. It is to be hoped that the accent of these languages be soon investigated for as Jagić truly remarks: "Ein tieferes Eindringen in die slavischen Betonungsverhältnisse ist für die endliche Lösung der Frage über die indo-germanische Betonung von grosser Wichtigkeit" and at another place: "Man muss vor allem an der slavischen Betonung und ihren Entwickelungsphasen die Einsicht in das Wesen des Accentes, in sein Verhältnis zur musikalischen Tonhöhe und Expirationsstärke, zur Quantität der Silbe zu gewinnen trachten."

In conclusion, it is my pleasant duty to express my warmest thanks to the following gentlemen: Professors Roman Brandt and Ph. Fortunatov of Moscow, Jan Baudouin de Courtenay and Lucian Malinowski of Cracow, Joseph Kallenbach and Wilhelm Streitberg of Freiburg i. S., for the valuable aid and instruction given me.

Common Abbreviations.

Obulg.	stands for		Old Bulgarian,
s.	„	„	Serbian,
lr.	„	„	Little-Russian,
sing.	„	„	singular,
pl.	„	„	plural,
part.	„	„	participle,
act.	„	„	active,
pass.	„	„	passive,
pers.	„	„	person,
pres.	„	„	present,
1st	„	„	first,
2nd	„	„	second,
3rd	„	„	third,
inf.	„	„	infinitive,
reg.	„	„	regular.

Bibliography. (Works of reference.)

A. Complete Russian-English Dictionary by A. Alexandrow. St.-Petersburg, 1885.

Начертаніе славянской акцентологіи. Сочиненіе Романа Брандта. Санктпетербургъ, 1880.

Лекціи по исторической грамматикѣ русскаго Языка, Романъ Грандтъ. Выпускъ I. Фонетика. Москва, 1892.

Лекціи по исторіи русскаго Языка. А. И. Соболевскаго. Изданіе второе. С.-Петербургъ, 1891.

Филологическія Разысканія Академика Я. К. Грота. Санктпетербургъ, 1873.

Akcenti u glagola. Od Gj. Daničića. Rad Iugoslavenske Akademije Znanosti i Umjetnosti. Knjiga VI. U Zagrebu, 1869.

Der Indogermanische Akzent. Ein Handbuch von Dr. Herman Hirt. Strassburg, 1895.

Leonhard Masing: Die Hauptformen des serbisch-chorwatischen Accentes. Mémoires de l'Académie Impériale des sciences de St.-Pétersbourg. T. XXIII No. 5. St. Pétersbourg, 1876.

De l'Accentuation du Verbe Russe par Paul Boyer. Paris, 1895.

Untersuchungen über Quantität und Betonung in den slavischen Sprachen.

I. Die Quantität im Serbischen. Von August Leskien. No II, VI. Leipzig, 1885, 1893.

Über den Accent der Verba im Kleinrussischen, von Dr. Clemens Hankiewicz, Archiv für Slavische Philologie, herausgegeben von V. Jagić. Zweiter Band, zweites Heft. Berlin, 1877.

The bibliography regarding the accent, phonology, morphology, etc. of the Slavonic languages is contained in Dr. Fr. Pastrnek's Supplement-Band zum Archiv f. Slavische Philologie. Berlin, Weidmannsche Buchhandlung, 1892. This bibliographical record of Slavonic philology for the last 15 years, should be the property of every university library in the United States. The "Anzeiger für indogermanische Sprach- und Altertumskunde redigiert von Wilhelm Streitberg" is also very valuable to the student of Slavonic philology.

Part First:

Simple Verbs with fluctuating accent.

As regards their accentuation, the Russian verbs fall into two groups. The one, and by far the larger of the two, accentuates the verbal forms, with few exceptions, on the same syllable upon which the accent bears in the infinitive. The smaller group is characterized by a shift of the stress from the syllable it strikes in the inf. to another in the other verbal forms. This shift which has its counterpart in the same process with the nominal flection creates four accent-types.

These types are:

A. The first person singular is oxytonic, the second pers. plural proparoxytonic and the other persons paroxytonic.

Example

$$\text{люби́ть: люблю́ \quad лю́бимъ}$$
$$\text{лю́бишь \quad лю́бите}$$
$$\text{лю́битъ \quad лю́бятъ.}$$

The numbers show which syllable is accented and this type may conveniently be expressed in the numerical formula $\frac{122 \quad 232}{\text{sing. \quad pl.}}$.

In the present and future tenses the verbs of this type bear the stress on the root-syllable except in the first pers. sing. which accentuates the personal ending.

B. The second pers. pl. is paroxytonic and the other persons are oxytonic.

Example

клясть: кляну́ кляне́мъ

кляне́шь кляне́те

кляне́тъ кляну́тъ.

The numerical formula of this type is: $\frac{111}{\text{sing.}} \frac{121}{\text{pl.}}$.

C. The first pers. sing. is oxytonic; the second pers. pl., paroxytonic and proparoxytonic, and the other persons oxytonic and paroxytonic.

Example

цѣни́ть: цѣню́ цѣни́мъ

цѣни́шь цѣни́те

цѣни́тъ цѣня́тъ.

The numerical formula combines therefore those of A and B: $\frac{122}{\text{sing.}} \frac{232}{\text{pl.}} + \frac{111}{\text{sing}} \frac{121}{\text{pl.}}$.

D. The second pers. pl. is proparoxytonic and the other persons are paroxytonic.

Example

часова́ть: часу́ю часу́емъ

часу́ешь часу́ете

часу́етъ часу́ютъ.

The numerical formula of this type is thus: $\frac{222}{\text{sing.}} \frac{232}{\text{pl.}}$.

The subdivisions of each of these types are based upon the morphological changes which the stem-finals undergo before the personal endings.

The stem finals may be divided according to Brandt's[1]) table of consonants into seven groups.

Their changes are as follows:

1. Labials: b, p; b + j (in ю = bl.[2])
   p + j   = pl.
2. Dentals: t, d; t + j = č[3]) or šč.[3])
   d + j = ž[4]) or žd (in Obulg. words).

---

[1]) Лекціи 107.   [2]) cf. Соболевскій 22.
[3]) cf. Соболевскій 22 and Grot 325.
[4]) cf. Соболевскій 21 and Grot 325.

3. Post palatals: ch, g, k; ch $+$ j $=$ š.

$$g + j = ž.$$
$$k + j = č.$$

4. Dento-labials: v, f; v $+$ j $=$ vl.

$$f + j = fl.$$

5. Dento-spirants: s, z; s $+$ j $=$ š.

$$z + j = ž.$$

6. Front palatals: š, ž, without change.

7. Nasals: m, n; m $+$ j $=$ ml.

8. The two groups of consonants: sk $+$ j $=$ šč.

$$st + j = šč.$$

Chapter I.

Present Tense.

Type A: $\frac{123}{\text{sing.}} \quad \frac{232}{\text{pl.}}$.

I. The stem (root) final is a labial: b, p.

a) The second stem (suffix) ends in — a —:

трепа́ть, to peel, strip (hemp), треплю́, тре́плешь.

щипа́ть, to pinch, щиплю́, щи́плешь.

In Malorussian, these verbs accentuate the suffix — a — of the inf.[1])

b) The second stem ends in — i —:

губи́ть, to destroy, гублю́, гу́бишь; s. gùbiti = *gubíti. s. gùbiti, gùbîm = *gubím, gubímo.

gùbîš	gubíte
gùbî	gùbê.

копи́ть, to heap, коплю́, ко́пишь.

лупи́ть, to pare, луплю́, лу́пишь; but s. lùpiti.

люби́ть, to love, люблю́, лю́бишь; s. ljúbiti = *ljūbíti. ljúbiti, ljûbîm, ljûbîš.

коробӣ́ть, to warp, короблю́, (его) коро́бить.

---

[1]) cf. Hankiewicz, Archiv, II, 292.

лѣпи́ть, to stick together, лѣплю́,[1]) лѣпишь; s. lijè-
piti (in the East: lépīti, in the West: lípiti) = *lēpíti,
accent like gùbiti.

руби́ть, to cut, рублю́, ру́бишь.

ступи́ть, to step, ступлю́, сту́пишь.

топи́ть,[2]) to heat, топлю́, то́пишь; s. tòpiti = *topíti.
tòpiti, tòpîm, tòpîš = *topíš.

труби́ть, to play thetrumpet, трублю́, тру́бишь;
s. trúbiti = *trūbíti. trúbiti, trúbîm, trúbîš, trúbî, trúbîmo,
trúbîte, trúbê. труби́ть also, but seldom follows type
$\frac{111}{} \frac{121}{}$.

цѣпи́ть, to clutch, цѣплю́, цѣпишь.

желоби́ть, to hollow, желоблю́, жело́бишь.

c) Second stem ends in — ě —:

терпѣ́ть, to suffer, терплю́, те́рпишь; s. tŕpjeti. tŕpjeti, tŕpîm, tŕpîš, tŕpî etc.

For Little-Russian, Hankiewicz[3]) gives the following
rules: Verba, deren Stamm auf $\overset{p,\ b}{\underset{s,\ z,\ v}{t, \quad d}}$ auslautet betonen im
Infinitiv, im ersten und zweiten Part. Perf. Act. die
Stammsilbe, in den übrigen die Personalendung oder
den Bindevocal. — Die ım Infinitiv auf êti auslautenden
Verba, deren Präsensstamm auf и (i) endigt, betonen nach
der Hauptregel IV[4]): Im Kleinrussischen besteht eine
durchgreifende Verschiedenheit zwischen der Bildung des
Präsens und den übrigen Formen des Zeitwortes. Zum
Präsensstamm gehört das Präsens, der Imperativ und
das Part. Praes. Act. Alles Übrige gehört zum zweiten
Stamm, dem Infinitivstamm.

Bei den Verben mit beweglichem Accent
braucht man also nur den Accent dieser beiden Stämme
zu kennen, um davon auf die Betonung der übrigen Zeit-
formen zu schliessen. Eine Ausnahme besteht nur beim

---

[1]) at Moscow one can hear also: лѣплю, but it is vulgar.
[2]) cf. Hirt. 201. [3]) H. Archiv, II, 291. [4]) cf. ibid and 290.

Imper. Praes. und dem Part. Perf. Pass. Der Imperativ
wird zwar aus dem Präsensstamm gebildet, hat aber die
Betonung des Infinitivs, das Part. Perf. Pass. wird aus dem
Infinitivstamm gebildet, hat aber die Betonung des Präsens.

II. The stem ends in a dental: t, d.

a) The second stem ends in — a —:

бормотáть, to murmur, бормочý, бормóчишь.

гоготáть, to cackle, гогочý, гогóчешь.

глодáть, to gnaw, гложý, глóжешь.

грохотáть, to rumble, грохочý, грохóчешь.

клеветáть, to slander, клевещý, клевéщешь.

клегтáть, клегчý, клѐгчешь.

клокотáть, to bubble, клокочý, клокóчешь: s. klo-
kòtati = *klokotáti, klòkoćêm, klòkoćêš, etc.

клохтáть, to cluck (of hens), клохчý, клóхчешь.

лепетáть, to lisp, лепечý, лепéчешь; s. lepètati =
*lepetáti, lèpećêm, lèpećêš, etc.

метáть, to throw, мечý and метáю, мéчешь and ме-
тáешь; s. mètati = *metáti, mètêm, mètêš, etc.

рокотáть, to roar, рокочý, рокóчешь.

роптáть, to grumble, ропчý, рóпчешь.

скрежетáть, to gnash, скрежещý, скрежéщешь.

стрекотáть, to chatter, стрекочý, стрекóчешь.

топтáть, to trample, топчý, тóпчешь.

трепетáть, to throb, трепещý, трепéщешь; s. tre-
pètati == *trepetáti, trèpećêm, trèpećêš, etc.

хлопотáть, to bustle, хлопочý, хлопóчешь.

хохотáть, to giggle, хохочý, хохóчешь.

шептáть, to whisper, шепчý, шéпчешь.

щебетáть, to warble, щебечý, щебéчешь.

щекотáть, to tickle, щекочý, щекóчешь.

b) Second stem ends in — i —:

будѝть,[1]) to wake, бужý, бýдишь; lr. будѝти, бýджу,
бýдишь; s. búditi = *būdíti, bûdîm, etc.

---

[1]) cf. Hirt. 201.

бродѝть, to ramble, брожу́, бро́дпшь; s. bròditi = *brodíti, bròdîm, bròdîš, etc.

водѝть, to lead, вожу́, во́дишь; s. vòditi = *vodíti, vòdîm, vòdîš, etc.

катѝть, to roll, качу́, ка́тпшь; it follows also type <u>111</u> <u>121</u> as one can hear at Moscow.

крутѝть, to twist, кручу́, кру́тишь; lr. крутѝти, кру́чу, кру́тпшь.

лудѝть, to tin, лужу́, лу́дпшь.

платѝть, to pay, плачу́, пла́ (ó) тпшь; it also follows type <u>111</u> <u>121</u>; s. plátiti, plâtîm, plâtîš, etc.

родѝть, to beget, рожу́, ро́дишь; s. ròditi = *rodíti. ròditi, ròdîm, ròdîš, ròdî, etc.

сердѝться, to grow angry, сержу́сь, се́рдишься; the accent of the inf. on the initial syllable is due to се́рдце.

судѝть, to judge, сужу́, су́дишь, lr. судѝти, су́джу, су́дпшь; s. súditi = *sūdíti. sûdîm, sûdîš. etc.

ходѝть, to walk, хожу́, хо́дишь; lr. ходѝти, хо́джу, хо́дпшь; s. hòditi = *hodíti, hòdîm, etc.

шутѝть, to joke, шучу́, шу́тишь. крестѝться,[1] крещу́сь, кре́стишься.

III. The stem ends in a postpalatal: ch, g, k.

a) Second stem ends in — a —:

дыха́ть, to breathe, дышу́, ды́шешь; s. díhati = *dīháti, dîšêm, dîšêš, etc.

пка́ть, to hickup, пчу́, пчешь, but more usual is: пка́ю пка́ешь, etc.

лока́ть, to lap, лочу́, ло́чешь, more frequently: лока́ю, лока́ешь, etc.

паха́ть, to plough, пашу́, па́шешь.

пыха́ть, to pant, пышу́, пы́шетъ.

Examples for the stem ending in — i — are wanting.

---

[1] cf. Grot 838.

IV. The stem ends in a dento-labial: v, f.

a) Second stem ends in — i —:

давить, to strangle, давлю, давишь; s. dáviti = *dāvíti; s. dáviti, dâvîm, dâvîš, etc.

ловить, to hunt, ловлю, ловишь; lr. ловити, ловлю, ловишь; s. lòviti = *lovíti. lòviti, lòvîm, lòvîš, etc.

травить, to graze, травлю, травишь; s. tráviti = *trāvíti, trâvîm, trâvîš, etc.

становить, to put, становлю, становвшь.

Examples for the stem ending in — a — are wanting.

V. The stem ends in a dento-spirant: s, z.

a) Second stem ending in — a —:

вязать, to tie, вяжу, вяжешь; lr. вязати, вяжу, etc.

писать, to write, пишу, пишешь; lr. pisáti, пишу, пишешь, пише etc.; s. písati = *pīsáti, pîšêm, pîšêš, pîšê, pîšêmo, pîšête, pîšû.

казать (у —), to show, кажу кажешь; lr. казати, кажу, кажешь; s. kázati, kâžêm, kâžêš, etc.

лизать, to lick, лижу, лижешь; lr. лизати, лижу, лижешь; s. lízati, lîžêm, lîžêš, etc.

лобзать, to kiss, лобжу, лобжешь, but also: лобзаю, etc.

низать, to string, нижу, нижешь; s. nízati, nîžêm, nîžêš, etc.

плясать, to dance, пляшу, пляшешь.

тесать, to hew, тешу, тешешь; lr. тесати, тешу, тешешь, etc.; s, tèsati = *tesáti, tèšêm, etc.

чесать, to comb, чешу, чешешь; lr. чесати, чешу, etc.; s. cèsati = *ćesáti, čěšêm, čěšêš, čěšê, etc.

b) Second stem ends in — i —:

бѣсить, to enrage, бѣшу, бѣсишь.

возить,[1]) to carry, вожу, возишь; lr. возити, вожу, возишь; s. vóziti = *vōzíti, vòzîm, vòzîš.

---

[1]) cf. Hirt. 200.

мѣси́ть, to knead, мѣшу́, мѣсишь; it follows also type B: <u>111</u> <u>121</u>. S. mijèsiti (E. mésiti, W. mísiti) = *mjēsíti, mijêsîm, mijêsîš, etc.

носи́ть, to bear, ношу́, но́сишь; lr. носи́ти, но́шу, но́сишь; s. nòsiti = *nosíti, nòsîm, nòsîš.

проси́ть,[1]) to ask, прошу́, про́сишь; s. pròsiti = *prosíti, pròsîm, pròsîš, pròsî, etc.

VI. The stem ends in a frontpalatal: š, ž.

a) Second stem is ending in — a —:

держа́ть, to hold, держу́, де́ржишь; s. dr̀žati = *dr̀žáti, dr̀žîm, dr̀žîš, dr̀žî, dr̀žû but držímo, držíte.

дыша́ть, to breathe, дышу́, ды́шишь.[2])

пыша́ть, to pant, пышу́, пы́шишь.[3])

b) Second stem in — i —:

души́ть, to choke, душу́, ду́шишь. In the sense of "perfuming", this verb is accented regularly: душу́, души́шь.

кружи́ть, to twirl, кружу́, кру́жишь, but it also may follow type B: <u>111</u> <u>121</u>.

служи́ть, to serve, служу́ слу́жишь; s. slúžiti = *slūžíti, slûžîm, slûžîš, slûžî, etc.

суши́ть, to dry, сушу́, су́шишь; s. súšiti = *sūšíti, sûšîm, sûšîš, sûšî, etc.

туши́ть, to extinguish, тушу́, ту́шишь; it also follows type B: <u>111</u> <u>121</u>; s, túšiti = *tūšíti, tûšîm, tûšîš.

VII. The stem ends in a nasal: m, n.

a) Second stem in — a —:

дрема́ть,[4]) to slumber; дремлю́, дре́млешь; s. drijèmati (E. drémati, W. drímati), drijêmlêm, drijêmlêš.

гнать,[5]) to drive, гоню́, го́нишь; lr. гна́ти, жену́, женёшь; s. gnàti, gnâm, gnâš, gnâ, gnàjû, but gnámo, gnáte.

b) Second stem in — и —:

гля́ну́ть, to look upon, гляну́, гля́нешь.

---

[1]) cf. ibidem 201.   [2]) cf. Sobolevskij 221 and Grot 328.
[3]) cf. Boyer 41.   [4]) cf. Hirt. 197.   [5]) cf. Grot 319.

мину́ть, to expire, мину́, ми́нешь, lr. мину́ти, reg. s. mínuti = *mīnúti, mînêm, mînêš, etc.

тону́ть,[1]) to founder, тону́, то́нешь; s. tònuti = *tonúti, tǒnêm, tonêš, tǒnê, tǒnêmo, tǒnête, tǒnû.

тяну́ть,[1]) to drag, тяку́, тя́нешь; lr. тягну́ти, reg.

The verbs ending upon — нути, are for the most part proparoxytones in Little-Russian and do not change their accent. [2])

c) Second stem in — i —:

дразни́ть, to tease, дразню́, дра́знишь.

жени́ться, to marry, женю́сь, же́нишься; s. žèniti = *ženíti, žěnîm, žěnîš, žěnî, etc.

клони́ть, to bow, клоню́, кло́нишь; s. klòniti = *kloníti, klònîm = *kloním, klònîš, klònî, klònê, but klonímo, klonite.

корми́ть, to nourish, кормлю́, ко́рмишь; s. kŕmiti = *kr̄míti, kr̂mîm, krmîš, etc.

ломи́ть, to break, ломлю́, ло́мишь; s. lómiti = *lōmíti, lòmîm, = *lomím, lòmîš, lòmî, lòmê, but lomímo, lomíte.

мѣни́ть, to change, мѣню́, мѣнишь, follows also type 111 121. s. mijèniti (E. méniti, W. míniti), mijênîm, mijênîš, etc.

VIII. The stem ends in a liquid: r, l.

a) Second stem in — a —:

ора́ть,[3]) to till, орю́, о́ришь; lr. ора́ти, орю, о́ришь; s. òrati = *oráti, ǒrêm, ǒrêš, ǒrê, ǒrêmo, ǒrête, ǒrû.

b) Second stem in — i —:

дѣли́ть, to divide, дѣлю́, дѣлишь; lr. дѣля́ти, дѣлю, дѣлишь; s. dijèliti = *djēlíti.

зубри́ть, to tooth, зубрю́, зу́бришь, follows also type 111 121.

мори́ть, to starve, морю́, мо́ришь, also according to type 111 121; s. mòriti = *moríti, mòrîm, mòrîš, etc.

---

[1]) cf. Hirt. 183. [2]) cf. Hankiewicz, Archiv, II, 295.
[3]) cf. Grot 327.

молѝть, to pray, молю́, мо́лишь; s. mòliti = *molíti, mòlîm, mòlîš, mòlî, etc.

пилѝть, to file, saw, пилю́, пи́лишь; s. pìliti = *pīlíti, pîlîm, pîlîš, pîlî, etc.

скоблѝть, to plane, скоблю́, ско́блишь, also follows type [111] [121].

сорѝть, to fill with dirt, сорю́, со́ришь, but also сорѝшь, сорѝтъ.

хвалѝть, to praise, хвалю́, хва́лишь; lr. хвалѝти, хвалю́, хвалѝшь, хвалѝтъ, хвалѧ́тъ, but хвалимо́, хвалите́; s. hváliti = *hvālíti, hvâlîm, hvâlîš, hvâlî, etc.

c) Second stem in — ě —:

смотрѣ́ть,[1] to look, смотрю́, смо́тришь; s. smòtriti, smòtrîm, smòtrîš, etc.

IX. The stem ends in: č, šč.[2]

a) Second stem — a —:

прыща́ть,[3] to fill with pimples, прыщу́, пры́щишь.

b) Second stem in — i —:

дрочѝть,   дрочу́, дро́чишь, also дрочѝшь, дрочѝтъ.

лечѝть, to cure, (лѣчѝть), лечу́, ле́чишь; s. léčiti, lijèčiti = ljèčíti, lêčîm, lêčîš, lêčî, etc.

лущѝть, to husk, лущу́, лу́щишь but also: лущѝшь, etc.

мочѝть, to moisten, мочу́, мо́чишь; s. mòčiti = *močíti, mòčîm, mòčîš, mòčî, mòčê but močímo, močíte.

сучѝть, to twist, сучу́, су́чишь, but also сучѝшь, сучѝтъ, etc.

тащѝть, to haul, pull, тащу́, та́щишь, also тащѝшь, etc.

точѝть, to grind, точу́, то́чишь; s. tòčiti = *točíti, tòčîm, tòčîš, tòčî, tòčê but točímo, točíte.

учѝть, to teach. учу́, у́чишь; s. ùčiti = *učíti, ùčîm = *učîm, ùčîš, ùčî, ùčê, but učímo, učíte.

---

[1] cf. Boyer 40.   [2] cf. Brandt: Лекцiи 117 ff.   [3] cf. Boyer 41.

X. The stem ends in st or sk.

Second stem in — a —:

хлестáть, to whip, хлещý, хлéщешь.

блистáть,[1]) to sparkle, блещý, блéщещь; s. blĭstati =
*blĭstáti, blĭstâm, blĭstâš, blĭstâ, blĭstajû but blĭstámo,
blĭstáte.

плескáть, to splash, плещý, плéщешь.

блескáть, to blaze, блещý, блéщешь.

искáть,[2]) to seek, ищý, и́щешь; s. ĭskati = *īskáti.

свистáть, to whistle, свищý, сви́щешь.

XI. Verbs with full vocalism (полногласіе.)[3]).

a) with rising accent = sharp (gestossen) accent in
Lithuanian:

борóться, to wrestle, *borti, борю́сь, бóрешься.

волóчь,[4]) to drag *velkti, волокý, волóчешь; lr. во-
лочи́, волóку and волóчу. In the Ukraina the inf. волокти́
is used.

колóть, to split, *kolti, колю́, кóлешь.

молóть,[5]) to grind, *melti, мелю́, мéлешь; s. mljèti.

полóть, to weed out, *pelti, полю́, пóлешь; s. pljèti,
plijèvem (East plévêm), plijèvêš, plijèvê, plijèvêmo, plijè-
vête, plijèvû.

порóть, to rip, *porti, порю́, пóрешь.

Examples with falling accent = soft (schleifend) accent
in Lith. are wanting.

b) The dissyllabism is unstressed:

волочи́ть, to trail, волочý, волóчишь; s. vlâčiti =
*vlāčíti, vlâčîm, vlâčîš, etc.; lr. волочи́ти, волóчу, волóчишь.

вороти́ть, to turn, ворочý, ворóтитъ.

голоси́ть, to speak loudly, голошý, голóсишь but
also голоси́шь, etc.; s. glásiti = *glāsíti.

---

[1]) cf. Grot 342.   [2]) cf. Hirt. 197 and 202.

[3]) Comp. Brandt: Лекцій 68 ff., Hirt: Der indogerm. Akzent
121—123 and Leskien: Unters. I, 550 ff.

[4]) cf. Sobolevskij 26.   [5]) cf. Hirt. 186 and 197.

городи́ть, to hedge in, горожу́, горо́дишь; s. гра́дити == *grādíti, grâdîm, grâdîš, etc.

золоти́ть, to gild, золочу́, золо́чишь, also золочи́шь; s. zlátiti == *zlātíti, zlâtîm, etc.

колоти́ть, to beat, колочу́, коло́тишь.

короби́ть, to bend, коробло́, коро́бить.

короти́ть, to shorten, корочу́, коро́тишь; s. krátiti == *krātíti, krâtîm, krâtîš, etc.

молоти́ть, to thrash, молочу́, моло́тишь; s. mlátiti == *mlātíti, mlâtîm, mlâtîš, etc.

полоска́ть, to rinse, полощу́, поло́щешь.

норови́ть, to watch an opportunity, норовло́, норо́вишь.

сторони́ться, to stand aside, сторонло́сь, сторо́ниться.

торопи́ть, to hasten, тороплю́, торо́пишь.

харони́ть, to hide, харонло́, харо́нишь.

The following verbs of this important class are added, though they have fixed accentuation, in order to facilitate the investigation of the polnoglasie question. Oxytones are:

борозди́ть, борони́ть, боронова́ть,ворова́ть, ворожи́ть, ворони́ть, вороти́ть,[1] вороши́ть, голода́ть, голосова́ть, дорожа́ть, дорожи́ть, колоси́ться, корот́ать, молоди́ть, молоде́ть, морокова́ть, мороси́ть, полосова́ть, полоши́ть, поло́щи́ть, пороси́ться, пороши́ть, солове́ть, солоди́ть, солоде́ть, солоне́ть, толо́чь, торопе́ть, торочи́ть, холоди́ть, холоде́ть, холости́ть, хорово́ди́ть, хороше́ть, шороши́ть.

Paroxytones are:

борода́вѣть, борода́тѣть, воро́чать, коро́стѣть, моро́зить, моро́чить, соро́мить, толо́чить, хорохо́риться, шоро́хнуть.

Proparoxytones are:

воро́бывать, коро́стовѣть, волоки́тствовать, холо́пствовать.

---

[1] it is of the perfective aspect; cf. Hirt. 200.

Oxytones are:

бередить, верезжать, верещать, деревянѣть, жеребиться, зеленѣть, пеленать, пеленговать, серебрить, чередить, шелестить, шелебить.

Paroxytones:

берéстить, мерéщить, тередóрить.

Tore Tornbiörnsson [1]) has sought to prove that the first vowel of the dissyllabisms oro, olo, ere, ele is secondary, while J. Schmidt, Fortunatov and others assert the contrary. None of the hypotheses thus far advanced explain the atonic character of the dissyllabism in words like: бородá, etc. Without assuming that I have found a solution, I venture to offer the following suggestion: In forming a verb from *gòṛd it would give gòṛd — i — ti and as the suffix of the first stem — i — drew the accent to it (cf. s. grádíti = *gradíti) we would have as a result, the form: goṛd — í — ti. Vocalic r was difficult to pronounce now and thus another o was interpolated between r and d, whereupon r lost its sonantic value. The noun was assimilated to the verb, therefore: gòṛd > gòrod. Where the first vowel is accented, there it seems most probable that it be primary.

XII. Special cases.

мочь,[2]) to be able: могý, мóжешь; lr. мочи́, мóгу, etc. The form мóжу, etc. also exists in Galicia and Bukovina.

In the Ukraina the infinitive моргти́ is heard; s. mòči, mògu, but mòžêš, mòžê, mòžêmo, mòžête, mògû.

хотѣть,[3]) to desire, хочý, хоти́мъ, хоти́те, хóчешь хóчетъ; lr. хотѣти, хóчу, etc.; хóчутъ but also хотя́тъ = Great-Russian хотя́тъ.

стлать,[4]) to spread, old. Bulg. стьлати, стелю́, стéлешь.

---

[1]) cf. Beiträge zur Kunde der indogermanischen Sprachen, XX, 181 ff.
[2]) cf. Grot 318, 338 and Sobolevskij 231. [3]) cf. Sobolevskij 221.
[4]) cf. Grot 328 and Hirt. 197.

The first and second persons pl. of the present tense
end in Little-Russian upon емо (емъ), еме or имо (имъ),
ите. If the first pers. sing. is oxytonic, the plural forms
are either paroxytonic: ємо (ємъ), єте or oxytonic: имо́
(имъ), итé.[1]) Imperfective verbs in Little-Russian are as
a rule paroxytones in the infinitive and the other verbal
forms except the past. part. pass.[2]) Verbs ending upon —
ати are mostly paroxytones and have fixed accentuation if
they retain the — a (— тв) in the present stem, otherwise
their accent recedes to the preceding syllable in the present tense. Verbs in Little-Russian whose second stem
ends in — и (i) — are for the most part paroxytones which
draw the accent to the preceding syllable in the present
tense. The proparoxytones ending in — ити have a fixed
accent. Mostly proparoxytonic are also those Little-Russian verbs which end in — нути. With the exception ·
of 6, all proparoxytones and paroxytones of this ending in
the inf., keep the latter's accentuation in the present tense.
The six exceptions bear the accent on the preceding, the
root syllable.[3])

As far as the few examples of Serbian and Malorussian
verbs compared with the Russian verbs of this type in the
present tense allow of an inference, the fact is worthy of
notice that both in Serbian a. Little-Russian the first person sing. bears the accent on the root-syllable while it is
oxytonic in Great-Russian. "Im Kleinrussischen, welches
in der Betonung des Verbums mehr vom Grossrussischen
abweicht als in der Betonung des Nomens, kommt ein
Wechsel in der Oxytonierung und Barytonierung der Präsensformen gar nicht vor, sondern es
herrscht eine stete Regelmässigkeit, dagegen findet häufig
ein Wechsel zwischen der Oxytonierung und Barytonierung

---

[1]) cf. Hankiewicz, Archiv, II, 291.   [2]) cf. idem, 290.
[3]) cf. Hankiewicz, Archiv, II, 295.

des Praesens und Praet. statt." [1]) In several cases, in Serbian the 1st u. 2nd pers. pl. are accented -ímo, -íte = īmó. īté and also Little-Russian knows this accentuation in -имó (ймъ), -итé when the first pers. sing. is oxytonic.[2]) Where Serbian has such accentuation as in bròdîm, bròdîš, lòmî, lòmê there the original accent fell upon the final syllable: *brodíš, *lomí, *lomé, etc.

In cases where in Serbian we find the accentuation of forms like trúbîm, trúbî, tŕpîš, there the original accent bore upon the second, the final syllable: *trubím, *trubí, *tŕpíš. This original oxytonization has become in Serbian paroxytonization which agrees with the present accentuation of the verbs of this type in Russian, except for the first person singular.

Type B: $\frac{111}{\text{sing.}}$ $\frac{121}{\text{pl.}}$.

To this type belong chiefly monosyllables which become dissyllabic in the present tense. They may be classified according to their root-vowel.

1. Root vowel: a.

брать, to take, берý, берёшь; lr. брáти, берý, берéшь, берé, берýтъ, but берéмо (ъ), берéте; s. bràti, bèrêm, bèrêš, bèrê, bèrêmo, berête, bèrû.

дать, to give, даю́, даéшь; lr. дáti, дамъ, дастъ, дамó, дастé, дадýтъ; s. dàti, dâm, dâš, dâ, but dámo, dáte, dádu.

звать, to call, зовý, зовёшь; lr. звáти, звý or зовý, зовéшь, etc. like брáти; s. zvàti, zòvêm, zòvêš, zòvê, zòvû but zovémo, zovéte.

класть, to lay, кладý, кладéшь; lr. (klásti), клáсти, кладý, кладéшь, etc.; s. klàsti, kládêm, etc.

клясть, to curse, кляну́, клянёшь, клянётъ, etc. s. kùnêm, kùnêš.

---

[1]) cf. Hankiewicz, Archiv, II, 289.   [2]) cf. ibidem 291.

пасть, to fall, паду́, падёшь; lr. (pásti) пáсти, паду́, -ёшь; s. pàsti, pádêm, pádêš, pádê, pádêmo, pádête, pádû.

2. The root-vowel is: e.

течь, to flow, теку́, течёшь; s. tèći, tèčêm, tèčêš, etc.

плесть, to braid, плету́, плетёшь; lr. плéсти, (плестú), плету́ -ёшь, -é, -у́тъ, but -éмо (мъ), -éте; s. plèsti, plètêm, plètêš, plètê, etc.

3. The root-vowel is: i.

гнить, to rot, гнію́, гніёшь; lr. гнúти, гнíю, гнúешь, etc.; s. gnjìti gnjìjêm, gnjìjêš, etc.

жить, to live, живу́, живёшь; lr. жúти, живу́, etc.; s. žívjeti, žívîm, žívîš, žívî, žívîmo, etc.

стричь, to shear, стригу́, стижёшь; lr. стрúчи; s. strìći, strìčêm, strìčêš, strìčê, etc.

4. The root-vowel is: ы.

грызть, to gnaw, грызу́, грызёмъ; lr. грúзти, грызу́, etc.; s. grìsti, grízêm, grízêš, etc.

плыть, to sail, плыву́, плывёшь; s. plìti, plìvêm, plì-vês, plìvê, etc.

5. The root-vowel is: ѣ.

пѣть, to sing. пою́, поёшь; s. pjèti, pòjêm, pòjêš, etc.

ѣсть, to eat, ѣмъ, ѣшь, ѣстъ, ѣдúмъ, ѣдúте, ѣдáтъ; lr. ѣмь, ѣсú, ѣсть, ѣмó, ѣсté, ѣдáтъ; s. jèsti, jêm, jêš, jê, jémo, jéte, jédû.

Here are only given those mostly in use, there are a few more of this type which are treated in the Archiv, V. 497 ff. by Prof. Leskien.

The more important dissyllables of this type are:

берéчь,[1] to take care of, берегу́, бережёшь;

(у)-мерéть, to die, (мру), мрётъ, мрутъ; s. mrijèti, (E. mréti, W. mríti), mrêm, mrêš, mrê, mrû, but mrémo, mréte; lr. merti, mru, mreš, mre, mrémo.

---

[1] Sobolevskij 53.

стере́чь, to guard, стерегу́, стережёшь; lr. стеречи́, and in the Ukraina: стерегти́.

тере́ть, to rub, тру, трёшь; lr. те́рти, тру, ешь, тре, труть, but тре́мо (мъ), тре́те; s. třti, trêm, trêš, trê. trû, but trémo, tréte.

These verbs are polnoglasie—verbs with the rising accent corresponding to the sharp intonation of the Lithuanian. Their accentuation of the root-syllable is Ur-Slavonic; бере́чь and стере́чь, make an exception.

While Great-Russian accents the last syllable except in the 2nd pers. pl. which is paroxytonic, Serbian shows several deviations from this rule but the old Serbian accentuation is also final in these cases; grízêm, pádê, plètêš = *grizém, *padế, *pletéš. As for the accent in Little-Russian it generally agrees with Great-Russian except in гни́ю, гни́ешь, etc.

Type C: $\frac{111}{\text{sing.}} \frac{121}{\text{pl.}} + \frac{122}{\text{sing.}} \frac{232}{\text{pl.}}$.[1]

I. The stem ends in a labial: b, p.

The second stem ends in —i—:

вопи́ть, to wail, воплю́, во́пишь;

долби́ть, to chisel, до́лбишь;

кропи́ть, to sprinkle, кроплю́, кро́пишь; s. kròpiti = *kropíti, kròpîm, etc., but kropímo, kropíte.

тупи́ть (ис —), to blunt, туплю́, ту́пишь; s. túpiti = *tūpíti, tûpîm, tûpîš, tûpî, etc.

II. The stem ends in a dental: t, d.

a) The second stem in —i—:

блуди́ть, to ramble, блужу́, блу́дишь; s. blúditi = *blūdíti, blûdîm, blûdîš, etc.

гнѣзди́ться, to nestle, гнѣзди́тъся; s. gnijèzditi (E. gnézditi) = *gnjēzdíti, gnjêzdî.

кади́ть, to incense, кажу́, ка́дишь; s. kádíti = *kādíti, kâdîm, kâdîš, etc.; lr. кади́ти, regular.

---

[1] cf. Grot 338 ff.

катить, to roll, качу, катишь.

коптить, to smoke, кончу, коптишь.

рядить, to hire, ряжу, рядишь.

садить, to sit, сажу, садишь; s. sáditi = *sādíti, sâdîm, sâdîš, etc.

светить,[1]) to light, свечу, светишь; s. svétiti = *svētíti, svêtîm, svêtîš, etc.

сладить, to sweeten, слажу, сладишь; s. sláditi, slâdîm, slâdîš, slâdî, etc.

студить,[2]) to cool, стужу, студишь; s. stúdjeti, stúdîm, stúdîš, stúdî, etc.

прудить, to stop up a dam, пружу, прудишь; s. prúdíti, = *prūdíti, prúdîm, prúdîš, etc.

трудиться, to work, тружусь, трудишься; s. trúditi = *trūdíti, trûdîm, etc.

цедить, to filter, цежу, цедишь; s. cijèditi = *cjēdíti, cjêdîm, cjêdîš, etc.

чертить, to sketch, черчу, чертишь.

удить, to angle, ужу, but also ужу, удишь; s. úditi = *udíti, údîm, údîš, etc.

b) Second stem in — ĕ —:

вертеть,[3]) to turn, верчу, вертишь; s. vŕtjeti = *vŕtjēti, vŕtîm, vŕtîš, etc.

III. The stem ends in a dento-labial: v, f.

a) The second stem ends in — a —:

плевать, to spit, плюю but also плюю, плюёшь.

b) Second stem in — i —:

травить, to graze, травлю, травишь, to graze.

In the sense of "hunting", this verb follows type D: $\frac{222}{sing.} \frac{232}{pl.}$; s. tráviti = *trāvíti, trâvîm, trâvîš, etc.

резвиться, to sport, резвлюсь, резвишься.

---

[1]) cf. Hirt. 201.   [2]) cf. Grot 339.   [3]) cf. Grot 338.

IV. The stem ends in a dento-spirant: s, z.

The second stem is — i —:

гасить, to extinguish, гашу́, га́сишь; lr. гасити, regular; s. gásiti = *gāsíti, gâsîm, gâsîš, etc.

грузи́ть, to sink, гружу́, гру́зишь.

коси́ть,[1] to mow, кошу́, ко́сишь; s. kòsiti = *kosíti, kòsîm, kòsîš, kòsî.

ме́сить, to knead, мешу́, ме́сишь; s. mijèsiti (E. mésiti, W. mísiti), mijêsîm, mijêsîš, etc.

(за) нози́ть, to get a splinter in, ножу́, но́зишь.

Here may be added the one verb whose stem ends in st:

крести́ть,[2] to christen, крещу́, кре́стишь; s. kŕstiti = *krstíti, kŕstîm, kŕstîš, etc., but krstímo, -íte.

V. The stem ends in a front-palatal: š, ž.

The second stem is — i —:

божи́ться, to swear, божу́сь, бо́жишься, but often божи́шься.

глуши́ть, to deafen, глушу́, глу́шишь.

души́ть, to choke, душу́, ду́шишь in the sense of "to stifle", but душу́, души́шь when it means "to perfume".

кроши́ть, to mince, крошу́, кро́шишь.

кружи́ть, to turn, кружу́, кру́жишь.

(по)ложи́ть,[3] to lay down, ложу́, ло́жишь; s. lòžiti = *ložíti, lòžîm, etc., but ložímo, ložíte.

суши́ть, to dry, сушу́, су́шишь; s. súšiti = sûšíti, sûšîm, sûšîš, sûšî.

туши́ть, to extinguish, тушу́, ту́шишь.

VI. The stem ends in a nasal: m, n.

The second stem is — i —:

мани́ть, to beckon, маню́, ма́нишь; s. mánjiti = *mānjíti, mânjîm, mânjîš, etc.

---

[1] cf. Grot 859.   [2] cf. Grot 888.   [3] cf. Hirt. 200.

(из)мѣни́ть, to change, мѣню́, мѣни́шь; s. mijèniti (E. méniti, W. míniti) = *mjēníti, mijênîm, mijênîš, etc.

лѣни́ться, to be idle, лѣню́сь, лѣни́шься; s. lijèniti se, (E. léniti se, W. líniti se), lijênîm, lijênîš, etc.

цѣни́ть, to value, цѣню́, цѣ́вишь; s. cijèniti = *cjēníti.

щени́ться, to pup, щени́тъся.

чини́ть, to do, чиню́, чи́нишь; s. čìniti = *čìníti, čìnîm, čìnîš, etc.; but činímo, činíte.

VII. The stem ends in a liquid: r, l.

Second stem ending in —‚i —:

вали́ть, to throw down, валю́, ва́лишь; lr. валѣ́ти, валю́, вали́шь; s. vàliti, vàlîm, vàlîš, etc.

вари́ть, to boil, варю́, ва́ришь; s. váriti = *vāríti, vârîm, vârîš, vârî, etc.

бѣли́ть, to bleach, бѣлю́, бѣли́шь; s. bijèliti (E. béliti, W. bíliti), bijêlîm, bijêlîš, etc.

дари́ть, to grant, дарю́, да́ришь.

дѣли́ть, to divide, дѣлю́, дѣли́шь; s. dijèliti (E. déliti, W. díliti) = djēlíti, dijêlîm, etc.

кури́ть, to perfume, курю́, ку́ришь.

мори́ть, to starve, морю́, мо́ришь; s. mòriti = *moríti, mòrîm, mòrîš, etc.; but morímo, -íte.

скобли́ть, to scrape, скоблю́, ско́блишь.

соли́ть, to salt, (соли́ть), солю́, со́лишь, but oftener соли́шь; s. sòliti = *solíti, sòlîm, etc.; but solímo, -íte.

тури́ть (вы-), to spur on, турю́, ту́ришь; s. tùriti, tùrîm, etc.

VIII. The stem ends in č and the second stem is —i —:

(раз) лучи́ть, to part, лучу́, лу́чишь; s. lúčiti.

(по) ручи́ть, to confide, ручу́, ру́чишь, oftener ручи́шь.

сучи́ть, to twist, сучу́, су́чишь.

IX. Special cases:

клеи́ть, to glue, клею́, кле́йшь, кле́йтъ, etc.

пои́ть, to water, пою́, по́йшь, по́ятъ.

The Serbian accentuation shows that the older accent bore upon the final syllable in numerous verbs of this type (cf.: stûdîš, vŕtî, etc.). The majority, however, of the Serbian verbs have the old accentuation of the root-syllable, f. i: trûdîš, trâvî, tûpîmo, etc. The Russian verbs of type C number 57 some of which like ручи́ть, соли́ть a. o. prefer type B: $\frac{111}{\text{sing.}}$ $\frac{121}{\text{pl.}}$. The number of verbs with double accent in the 2nd $+$ 3rd pers. sing. and in the pl. is therefore not considerable. It is natural to suppose that originally they were accented according to type B and that through the prevalence of type A: $\frac{122}{\text{sing.}}$ $\frac{232}{\text{pl.}}$ they have gradually adopted the accentuation of type A while still retaining that of type B.

Type D: $\frac{222}{\text{sing.}}$ $\frac{232}{1^{\text{r.}}}$.

To this type belongs the numerous class of frequentatives upon -овать, -евать. They are for the most part denominatives and deverbatives whose verbal stem ends upon -u (-ov-) which is accented in all verbal forms. This is not only the case in Russian but in all Slavonic languages. They are oxytonic in the inf., except: тре́бовать, рафини́ровать and дамаски́ровать. The last two owe their accentuation on the antepenultimate to their German originals in -íren which again are formed from French verbs upon -er. Many of the verbs upon -овать, -евать are loanwords and their number is steadily increasing. The first person either ends in -у́ю or in -ю́ю.

Examples: рисова́ть, to design.

рису́ю   рису́емъ
рису́ешь   рису́ете
рису́етъ   рису́ютъ

воева́ть, to make war: вою́ю   вою́емъ
вою́ешь   вою́ете
вою́етъ   вою́ютъ.

A few more form their present tense, like воевать.

They are: горевáть, малевáть, and передневáть. The other verbs upon -евáть and all upon -овáть follow the example of рисовáть. Those verbs which are not oxytonic in the inf., like the 3 above-mentioned and гарантúровать, accent the same syllable in the varions verbal forms. But all oxytonic infinitives accentuate the — ý — or — ю́ —. The other forms are accented as follows:

Imperative: -ýй, -ýйте.
Part. pres. act.: -ýющiй.
Part. pres. pass.: -ýемъ, -ýемiй.
Gerund: -ýя.
Past part. pass.: -óванъ, -óванный.

The Little-Russian verbs of this ending agree with the Great-Russian verbs in regard to their accentuation. In Serbian, this class of verbs may be illustrated by: kupòvati = *kupováti, to buy. kùpujêm, kùpujêš, kùpujê, kùpujêmo, kùpujête, kùpujê.

Imperative: kùpûj, kùpûjmo, kùpûjte.
Part. pres. act.: kùpujûći = *kupújūći.

For Little-Russian, Hankiewicz formulates the following rule: "Die auf obamu auslautenden Verba haben im Infinitiv den Accent entweder auf der viert- oder zweitletzten Silbe. Im ersteren Falle haben sie unbeweglichen Accent, im letzteren Falle wird die Silbe ва oder y, welche an die Stelle von ова tritt, betont, z. B. куповáти, купу́ю, купу́ючiй, куповáвши. [1])

Another group of the verbs following type D are 12 verbs upon -áть, viz:

алкáть, to be hungry, áлчу, áлчешь, but also regularly: алкáю, but áлкаешь, etc.

брехáть, [2]) to bark, брешу́, брéшешь, брéшутъ.

зобáть, to peck, зóблю, зóблешь.

зыбáть, [3]) to swell, move, зы́блю, зы́блешь; зыблю́ occurs also.

---

[1]) cf. Archiv II, 296.   [2]) cf. Grot 382.   [3]) cf. ibidem.

имáть (изъ-), to take out, -éмлю, -éмлешь, -éмлютъ.

колебáть, to swing, колéблю, колéблешь.

колыхáть, to shake, колы́шу, колы́шешь; колышу́ is also heard, as well as колыхáю.

стонáть,[1]) to sigh, стóну and стону́, стонáю, стóнешь, стóнутъ.

страдáть, to suffer, стрáжду and страдáю, etc.

хромáть, to limp, хрáмлю and хромáю, etc.

The first pers. sing of брехáть, колыхáть and стонáть is rather oxytonic than paroxytonic; this is at least the case at Moscow. It is a fact worth noticing that the accentuation varies in the different parts of Russia and that the higher classes prefer sometimes a different accentuation from that which prevails among the lower classes. This circumstance may also account to some extent for the double accentuation of type C.

Chapter II.

Future Tense.

The following verbs are oft the perfective aspect i. e. they express in the form of the present tense[2]) the action of the future. Those treated in Chap. I. are imperfective verbs, their action continues yet while we are speaking of it. The perfective verbs may also be called resultative verbs since their meaning implies the attaining of an end. Imperfective verbs become perfective by using them with a prefix. Since their present form expresses future action, the resultative verbs have neither a present participle nor a present gerund. Some of the verbs with the perfective aspect are simple but the majority of them are only used with a prefix which in cases like снять, обязáть is no longer felt to be such. They are now considered simple verbs.

---

[1]) cf. Hirt. 197 and Boyer 15.   [2]) Comp. Sobolevskij 228.

Type A: $\frac{132}{\text{sing.}}\ \frac{232}{\text{pl.}}$.

I. The verbal stem ends in a labial, the second stem is
— i —:

купи́ть, to buy, куплю́, ку́пишь; lr. купи́ти, ку́плю, ку́пишь; s. kúpiti = *kūpíti, kûpîm, kûpîš, kûpî, etc.

ступи́ть, to walk, ступлю́, сту́пишь.

(под-), пособи́ть, to assist, пособлю́, посо́бишь.

(у)- цѣпи́ть, to chain, уцѣплю́, уцѣпишь.

II. The stem ends in a dental and the second stem is
— i —:

проглоти́ть, to swallow, проглочу́, проглóтишь.

об(в)ороти́ть, to turn, оборочу́, оборóтишь.

хвати́ть, to seize, хвачу́, хвáтишь; s. hvàtiti, a shortened on account of rising accent, xbàtîm, xbàtîš, etc.

III. The stem ends in a postpalatal or in sk, st.

a) Second stem is — a —:

скака́ть, te jump, скачу́, скáчешь; s. skákati, skâčêm.

сыска́ть, to search, сыщу́, сы́щешь, сы́щутъ.

b) Second stem is — i —:

пусти́ть, to let go, пущу́, пýстишь; lr. пусти́ти, пýщу, пýстишь; s. pùstiti = *pustíti, pùstîm, pùstîš, pùstî, etc.

IV. The stem ends in a front palatal: ž.

одолжи́ть, to lend, oblige, одолжу́, одóлжишь.

V. The stem ends in a nasal: m, n.

a) Second stem is — u —:

обману́ть,[1]) to deceive, обману́, обмáнешь.

помяну́ть,[1]) to mention, помяну́, помя́нешь.

b) Second stem is — i —:

(за-) урони́ть, to drop, уроню́, урóнишь; s. ròniti, rònîm, rònîš, but ronímo, roníte.

ошеломи́ть, to stupefy, ошеломлю́, ошелóмишь.

---

[1]) cf. Hirt. 188.

прислони́ть, to lean against, прислоню́, присло́-
нишь; s. prislòniti = slonìti, prislònîm, etc., but prislo-
nímo, -íte.

VI. The stem ends in a dento-spirant or č.

(за-), укуси́ть, to bite, укушу́, уку́сишь; s. za-kúsiti,
за-kûsîm, etc.

обвяза́ть, to oblige, обяжу́, обя́жешь.

соскочи́ть, to jump down, соскочу́, соско́чишь.

VII. Special case.

в-, при-, об-, от-, под-, с-н-ять; to take down;
-ять is of the imperfective aspect, -имать is its frequenta-
tive form.

сниму́, сни́мешь etc., сни́мутъ.

Type B: $\frac{111}{\text{sing.}} \frac{121}{\text{pl.}}$.

вз-ять, to take, возьму́, возьмёшь, возьмётъ, возь-
му́тъ.

(при-) обрѣ́сть, to find, discover, обрѣту́, обрѣ́тешь,
обрѣ́тётъ, обрѣту́тъ.

сопря́чь, to join in matrimony, сопрягу́, сопряжёшь,
сопряжётъ.

сѣчь, to chop, сѣку́, сѣчёшь, сѣчётъ.

умере́ть, to die, умру́, умрёшь; s. ùmrijeti (E. úm-
rêti, W. ùmrîti), ùmrêm, ùmrêš, ùmrê etc.

Type C: $\frac{122}{\text{sing.}} \frac{232}{\text{p}^1} + \frac{111}{\text{sing.}} \frac{121}{\text{pl.}}$.

облокоти́ться, to lean one's elbow on, облокочу́сь,
облоко́тишься.

отвори́ть, to open, отворю́, отво́ришь.

яви́ть, to show, явлю́, я́вишь; s. jáviti = *jāvíti, jâvîm,
jâvîš, jâvî, etc.

It is very difficult at times to determine whether a perfective verb is to be regarded as a simple or composed verb;
therefore those verbs which are not mentioned here, will
be treated together with the composed verbs.

Chapter III.

Imperative.

The rule in this verbalform is that the modal suffix-i (й) bears the accent. The infinitive being oxytonic, the imperative and the 1st pers. sing. are also oxytonic except where the latter follows type D. The forms of the imperative are grouped according to the accent type which the respective infinitive follows.

$$\text{Type A}: \frac{122}{\text{sing.}} \frac{232}{\text{pl.}}$$

(за-) вяжи́ (за·) куси́ звони́ бори́сь броди́ бѣси́ (за-) кажи́ (за-) нози́ золоти́ бреши́ буди́ вними́ вози́ вороти́ городи́ клегчи́ дави́ волочи́ гони́ грохочи́ губи́ гогочи́ держи́ s. dřži, (по-) ложи́, дразни́, души́, дыши́, жени́сь, ищи́, клевещи́, клокочи́, клони́, колоти́, коли́, колыши́, копи́, корми́, короти́, коси́, крести́сь, крути́, купи́, кури́, лепечи́, лобжи́, лови́, ломи́, луди́, лупи́, лечи́ (лѣчи́), люби́, мечи́ (мета́ть), мини́, молоти́, мели́, мочи́, моги́, [1]) норови́, носи́, обмани́, обними́, обяжи́, одолжи́, ори́, ошеломли́, паши́, пиши́, плати́, плещи́, пляши́, поглоти́, подсоби́, полощи́, поли́, получи́, помяни́, пори́, пособи́, прими́, прислони́, проглоти́, проси́, пусти́, пыши́, подыми́, подними́, роди́, рокочи́, ропщи́, руби́, свищи́, серди́сь, скачи́, -скочи́, служи́, смотри́, сними́, станови́, стели́, ступи́, суди́, суши́, терпи́, теши́, тони́, s. tòni = *toní, топи́, топчи́, торопи́, точи́, трепещи́, тужи́, тяни́, урони́, учи́сь, хвали́, хвати́, хлещи́, хлопочи́, ходи́, хорони́, хоти́, хохочи́, цѣпи́сь, чеши́, шути́, щебечи́, щекочи́, дремли́.

The Serbian imperative has generally the secondary accent, f. i.: lòmi = *lomí, kólji = *koljí, òri = *orí, píši = *pīší, plijèvi = *plijeví.

$$\text{Type B}: \frac{111}{\text{sing.}} \frac{121}{\text{pl.}}$$

бери́,	клани́,	три́,	обрѣти́
возьми́,	сѣки́,	теки́,	умри́
грызи́,	стереги́,	перегряги́,	зови́.
живи́,	стриги́,	плети́	-бреги́
клади́,	пади́,	плыви́.	

---

[1]) cf. Sobolevskij 227.

In Serbian, the secondary accent prevails; bèri =
*berí, zòvi = *zoví, žívi = žīví, ùmri and mrì.

Type C.

бѣлѝ, валѝ, варѝ, вертѝ, вопѝ, часѝ,

голосѝ,	кропѝ,	свѣтѝ,	турѝ.
грузѝ,	кружѝ,	скоблѝ,	тушѝ.
(за-) глушѝ,	манѝ,	сладѝ,	уѣдѝ.
дарѝ,	мѣнѝ,	слѣпѝ,	цѣнѝ.
дѣлѝ,	мѣсѝ,	студѝ,	чертѝ.
	морѝ,	сучѝ,	чинѝ.
кадѝ,	пой,	тащѝ,	шевелѝ.
катѝ,	рѣзвѝсь,	трубѝ, s. trúbi,	шепчѝ.
клей,	рядѝ,	трудѝсь,	явѝсь.
коптѝ	садѝ,	-тупѝ.	

In Little-Russian, for the verbs with movable accent
the following rule holds: "Der Imperativ wird zwar aus
dem Präsensstamm gebildet, hat aber die Betonung des
Infinitivs". [1]) The same rule, as we have seen, holds good
in Great-Russian, with the following exceptions, viz.

1) The imperative is paroxytonic:
зыбли, приемли.   Грузѝ also belongs to this
колебли, трепли. group, but it is also oxytonic.

2) The modal suffix is atonic: ь in
ичь by side of икай, and удь (удѝть), as well as generally in those cases where it follows a vowel, vg.: дай, пой
s. pôj, алкай.

Chapter IV.

Gerund.

Many verbs are lacking in this verbal form even then,
when the aspect or mode allows of this form. [2]) The rule is
the oxytonization.

The oxytonic gerunds are:

---

[1]) cf. Hankiewicz Archiv, II, 291.
[2]) comp. Grot 330 and Sobolevskij 232 ff.

Type A.

бродя́, дыша́, коля́, оря́, свистя́,
дава́, ища́, кося́, ропща́. терпя́,
водя́, гоня́, любя́, стеля́, топча́,
дремля́, крутя́, меля́, служа́, (про)ходя́.

Type B.

беря́, грызя́, кладя́, плывя́,
зовя́, живя́, кляня́, ѣдя́.

Type C. has вертя́, Type D. бреша́.

Paroxytones:

страда́я type D., прие́мля type D., (по) хра́мывая (B) and тре́буя are proparoxytonic, the latter agreeing with its proparoxytonic infinitiv; хва́ля (A)

This list comprises only the most common gerunds; as a rule this verbal form is avoided in the daily conversation and only poets and romance-writers patronize it.

Chapter V.

Present Participle Active.

This form is proparoxytonic bearing the accent as a rule on the root syllable, only the following are paroxytonic, accenting the suffix, viz.:

Type A.

могу́щій s. mŏgûći, бродя́щій; both are rather neuter than active.

Type B.

грызу́щій, but part. past. гры́зшій.
кладу́щій,
кляну́щій,
берегу́щій, but part. past. бере́гшій.
беру́щій, s. bĕrûći.
плыву́щій,
стерегу́щій,
теку́щій.

This verbal form is also more of a book form the accentuation of which oscillates in several cases.

Chapter VI.

Past Participle Passive.

The rule is: The shortened form of this participle ending in the masculine gender upon -анъ, -янъ, -енъ, -ѣнъ, -емъ, -отъ and -утъ bears the accent on the preceding syllable, and is therefore paroxytonic while its full ending upon -анный, -янный, -енный, -ѣнный,[1] -отый and -утый is proparoxytonic. There are a few oxytonic forms not only in the masculine gender, but also in the feminine and neuter as well as in the plural. These oxytonic participles are:

Type A.

(по бужденъ, á, ó, ѝ.
одолженъ, á, ó, ѝ.
окруженъ, á, ó, ѝ.
(от) мѣненъ, á, ó, ѝ.
ошеломленъ, á, ó, ѝ.
рожденъ, á, ó, ѝ.
сужденъ, á, ó, ѝ.
учёнъ, á, ó, ѝ but s. ũčen.

Type B.

бережёнъ, á, ó, ѝ.
сопряжёнъ, á, ó, ѝ.
стережёнъ, á, ó, ѝ.
сѣчёнъ, á, ó, ѝ.

Grot 321 accentuates сѣченъ but at Moscow this accentuation is entirely unknown.

обрѣтёнъ has a double accent in the masculine gender, but is oxytonic in the fem., neuter and plural forms.

For Little-Russian, Hankiewicz[2] formulates the follo-

---

[1] On the orthography of these endings comp. Sobolevskij 234.
[2] cf. Archiv, II, 291.

wing rule: das Part. Perf. Pass. wird aus dem Infinitivstamm gebildet, hat aber die Betonung des Präsens, z. B.
писа́ти, пи́санный; according to the 1st pers. sing. pres.
tense: пишу́. If therefore, the 1st pers. sing. present be
paroxytonic, the past part. pass. will be paroxytonic in its
shortened predicative form upon -анъ and proparoxytonic as
in Great-Russian in its full ending upon -анный. This rule
holds good for the verbs with movable accent in both the
Great- and Little-Russian (languages) dialects. [1]

Chapter VII.

Past Participle Active.

This participle reproduces regularly the accentuation
of the infinitive. The feminine, neuter and plural forms
are then paroxytonic. Several verbs, however, have either
one or two or even all three last-named forms oxytonic
and agree therefore with the oxytonic infinitive.

Type A.

гнала́, о́ but гна́ли.
могла́, о́, и́; s. mŏgao, but mògla, mòglo.

Type B.

брала́ but also бра́ла, брало́ but бра́ли; s. brăo but
bràla.
взяла́, but взя́ло, взя́ли.
берёгъ, берегла́, берегло́.
звала́, but зва́ло, зва́ли; s. zvă but zvála.
грызла́, [2] but гры́зло, гры́зли.
дала́, дало́ but да́ли.
жила́, but жи́ло, жи́ли.
клала́, клало́, клали́.
облекла́, облекло́, облекли́.
обрѣла́, обрѣло́, обрѣли́.

---

[1] comp. also ibidem 291, rule VI.
[2] Grot 320 accentuates гры́зла but this contradicts the usage of
Moscow.

н.

низа́ть 16.
(за)-нози́ть 28.
норови́ть 21.
носи́ть 17.

о.

облокоти́ться 34.
обману́ть 33.
обороти́ть 33.
обрѣ́сть 34.
обля́ть 34.
одолжи́ть 33.
ора́ть 18.
отвори́ть 34.
ошеломи́ть 33.

п.

пасть 24.
паха́ть 15.
пили́ть 19.
писа́ть 16.
плати́ть 15.
плева́ть 27.
плеска́ть 20.
плесть 25.
плыть 25.
пляса́ть 16.
по́йть 29.
полоска́ть 21.
поло́ть 20.
помяну́ть 33.
поро́ть 20.
пособи́ть 33.
прислони́ть 34.
проглоти́ть 33.
проси́ть 17.
пруди́ть 27.

прыща́ть 19.
пусти́ть 33.
пыха́ть 15.
пыша́ть 17.
пѣть 25.

р.

роди́ть 15.
рокота́ть 14.
ропта́ть 14.
руби́ть 13.
ручи́ть 29.
рѣзви́ться 27.
ряди́ть 27.

с.

сади́ть 27.
свиста́ть 20.
свѣти́ть 27.
серди́ться 15.
скака́ть 33.
скобли́ть 19. 29.
скрежета́ть 14.
слади́ть 27.
служи́ть 17.
смотрѣ́ть 19.
снять 34.
соли́ть 29.
сопря́чь 34.
сори́ть 19.
соскочи́ть 34.
станови́ть 16.
стерѣ́чь 26.
стлать 22.
стона́ть 32.
сторони́ться 21.
страда́ть 32.
стрекота́ть 14.

стричь 25.
студи́ть 27.
ступа́ть 13. 33.
суди́ть 15.
сучи́ть 19. 29.
суши́ть 17. 28.
сыска́ть 33.
сѣчь 34.

т.

тащи́ть 19.
терѣ́ть 26.
теса́ть 16.
течь 25.
тону́ть 18.
топи́ть 13.
топта́ть 14.
торопи́ть 21.
точи́ть 19.
трави́ть 16. 27.
трепа́ть 12.
трепета́ть 14.
труби́ть 13.
труди́ться 27.
тупи́ть 26.
тури́ть 29.
туши́ть 17. 28.
тяну́ть 18.

у.

уди́ть 27.
укуси́ть 34.
умерѣ́ть 34.
урони́ть 33.
учи́ть 19.

х.

хвали́ть 19.
хвати́ть 33.

хлеста́ть 20.
хлопота́ть 14.
ходи́ть 15.
хорони́ть 21.
хотѣ́ть 22.
хохота́ть 14.
хрома́ть 32.

ц.

цѣди́ть 27.
цѣни́ть 29.
цѣпи́ть 13. 33.

ч.

черти́ть 27.
чеса́ть 16.
чини́ть 29.

ш.

шепта́ть 14.
шути́ть 15.

щ.

щебета́ть 14.
щекота́ть 14.
щени́ться 29.
щипа́ть 12.

ѣ.

ѣсть 25.

я.

яви́ть 34.

Типографія (Липпертъ и Ко.) Г. Пеца, Наумбургъ и/С.

CPSIA information can be obtained
at www.ICGtesting.com
Printed in the USA
BVHW071252311218
536776BV00014B/2171/P